Creative Reading & Writing

Book 3A

The Short ĭ Sound

Contents

- Building Vocabulary with Phonics
- Identifying Vowels
- Reading 3 and 4-letter words
- Practicing Sight Words
- Reading & Writing Stories
- Drawing & Colouring
- Cut & Paste Activities
- Rhyming Words
- Numbers & Puzzles
- Mazes & Word Games
- Colours and Shapes
- Introducing Y as the long i sound.
- Quiz and Word List
- Teaching Tips and more!

No part of this book may be reproduced in any form or stored in any retrieval system without the permission of the publisher.

Copyright ©2024FayeClunies-Ross

Box 5449 Haines Junction, Yukon, Canada
Y0B1L0

www.canyoncountryfarms.ca

©FayeClunies-Ross

Creative Reading And Writing Book 3A

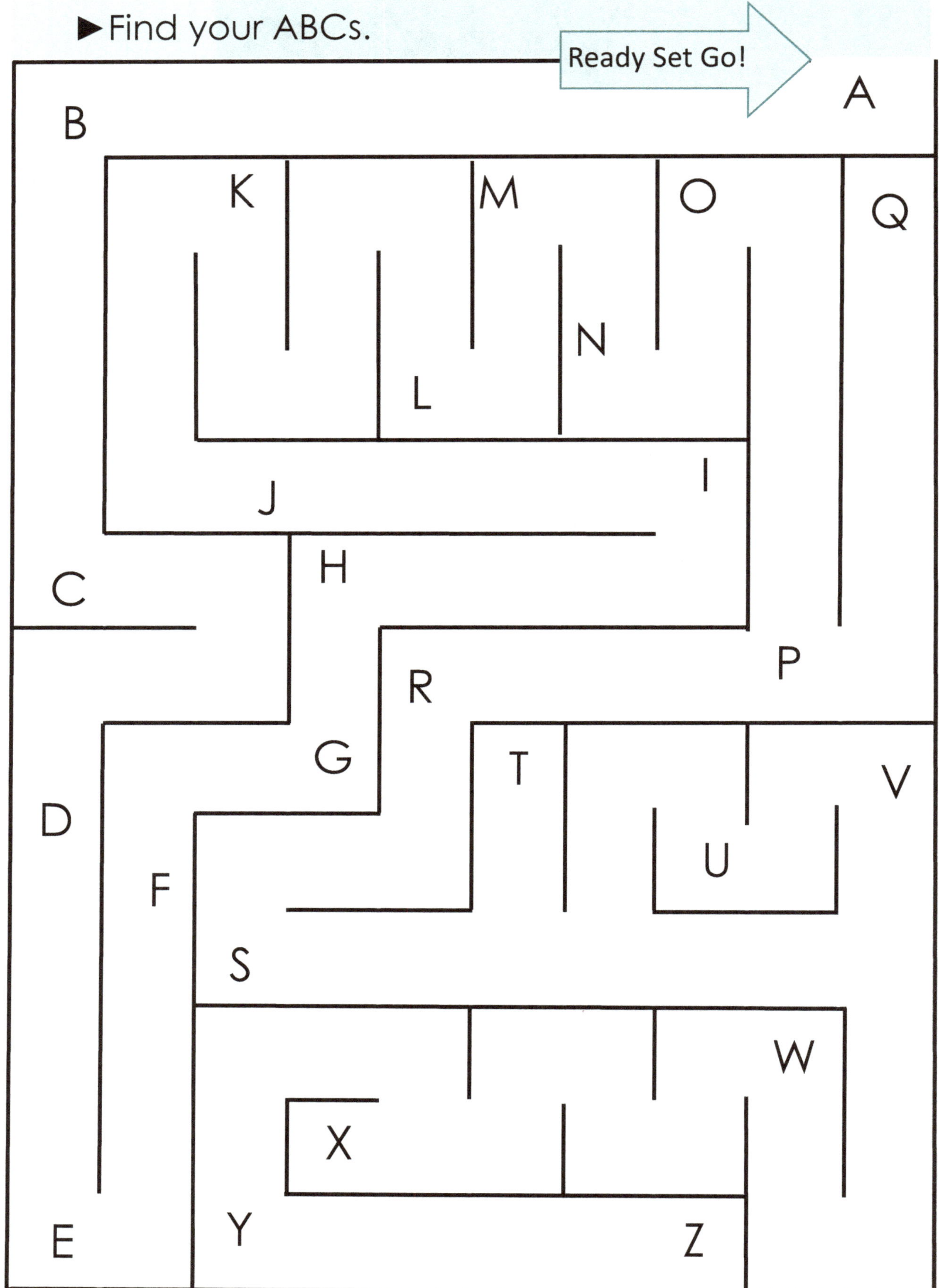
Ready Set Go!
A
B
K
M
O
Q
N
L
I
J
H
C
P
R
G
T
V
D
U
F
S
X
W
E
Y
Z

▶ Write the alphabet.

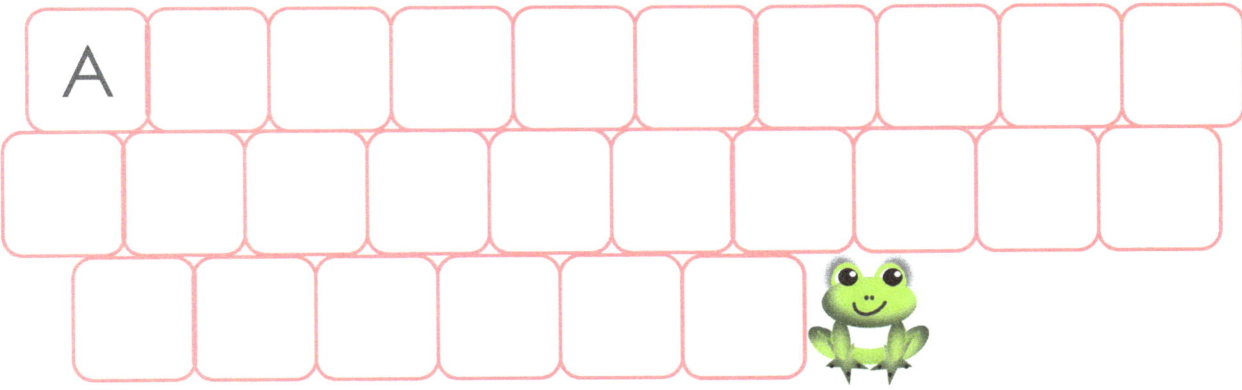

▶ Play 3-in-a-row, tic tac toe.

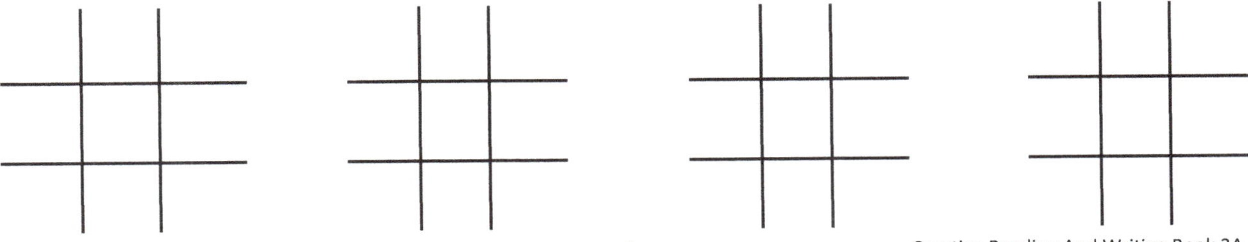

Ii

▶Say the ĭ sound in **pig**...ĭ... ĭ... ĭ.

▶Circle the letters, **I i**.

```
i  h  b  t  c  i  d  h  i  v  a  f  k  a  s  I
h  w  e  i  I  j  e  k  a  l  o  u  p  m  n  o
a  q  o  u  r  s  E  A  t  u  v  p  i  E  t  A
l  I  x  e  A  y  t  I  z  a  I  q  p  r  k  a
y  c  z  i  o  a  A  q  p  u  O  t  i  a  e  q
i  e  s  E  u  A  I  u  e  f  w  n  E  s  z  i
```

▶Circle the noun in each box. (a person or thing)

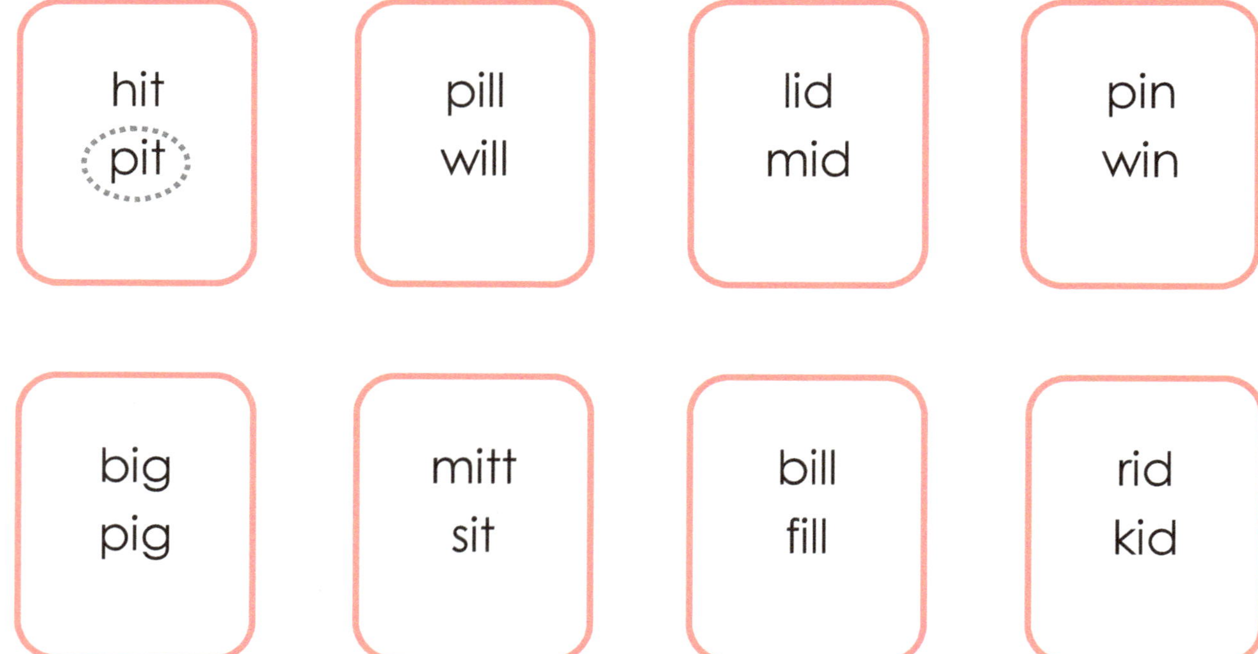

► Write the vowels on the blocks.
► Say the short vowels sounds... ă, ĕ, ĭ, ŏ, ŭ.

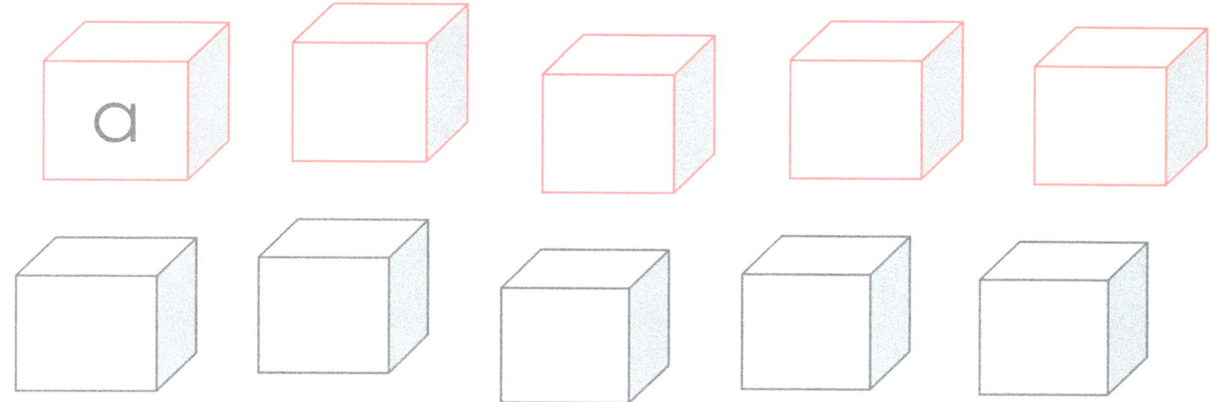

► Match the sounds.

a .... nun

e   mat

i   Tom

o   pet

u   tin

a   sin

e   lap

i   fun

o   pop

u   men

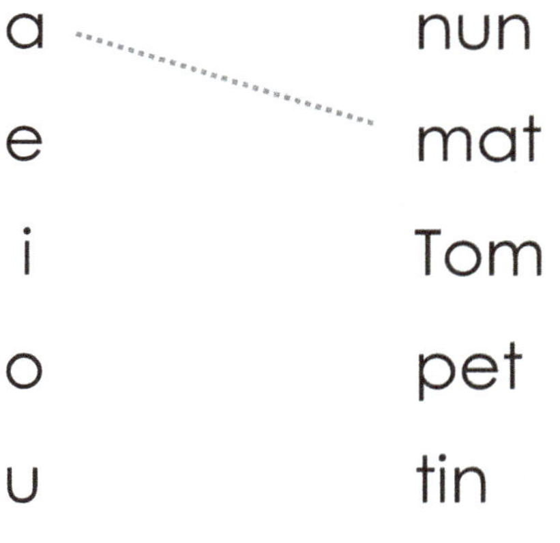

► How many vowels
   are in each word?

pin	1
pine	
tin	
teen	
mini	
in	
bin	
bind	

► Draw a picture for each word.

fig

pig

wig

twig

► Read the story. Check a box. What rhymes with ig?

The Big Pig

This is a pig.

This is a big pig.

The pig likes to sit.

The pig likes to eat.

He likes to eat pig feed.

He likes to eat figs!

The big pig will eat and eat.

dig

©FayeClunies-Ross

► Write a story. Draw a picture of your story.

<u>At the Farm</u>

One day ...

____

____

____

____

____

____

► Read and rewrite new words.

farm			
feed			
eat			

Ii

says, **i**, as in white

says, **ĭ**, as in mint

▶ What colour is it?

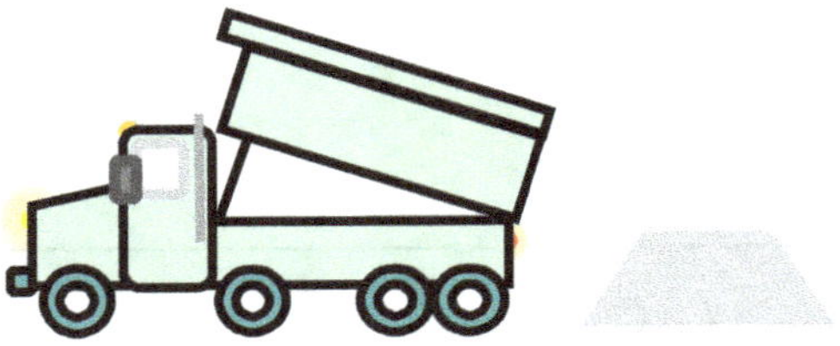

▶ What colour is it?

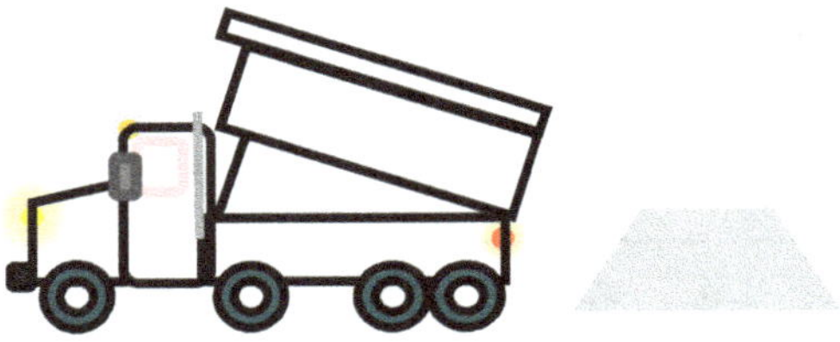

▶ Finish the sentence with a colour word.

The	little		lamb	has

nice	soft		wool.

▶ How many words can you find?

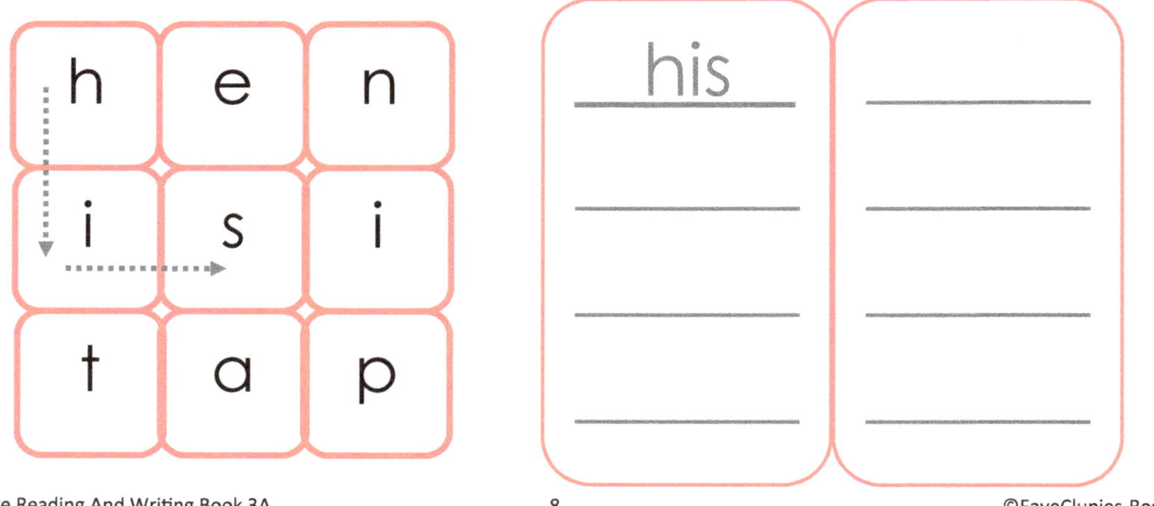

h	e	n
i	s	i
t	a	p

his

►My name is __________________________

Home

1	2	3
4	5	6
7	8	9
*	0	#

►My phone number.

____ ____ ____ - ____ ____ ____ ____

►My address.

____

____

____

►Match colours.

black	
amber	
red	

mint	
white	
tan	

►What rhymes?

ig

►Circle the vowels. Write how many.

Goat Farm	
Sheep pasture	
Hay bales	

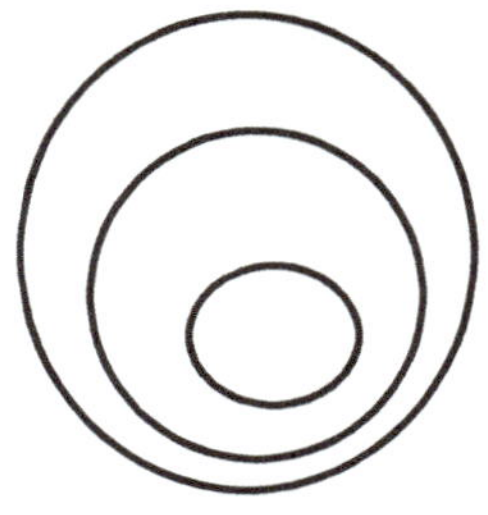

body and head

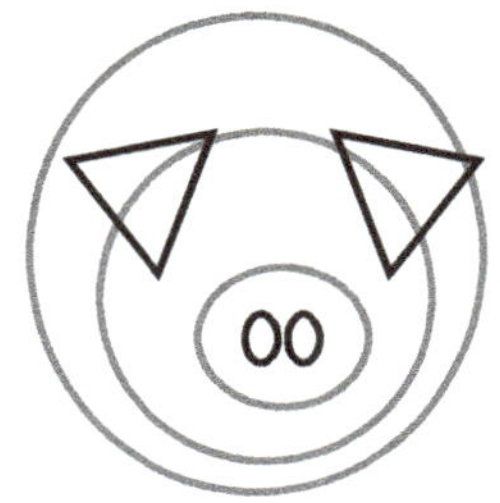

nose and ears

feet and tail

eyes and toes

colour

shade

► Draw a pig.

► What would you name a pet pig?

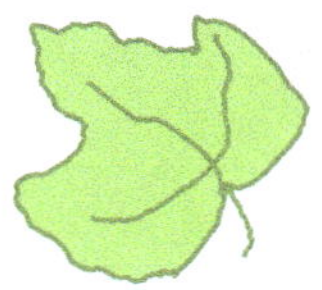

____

► Match and write new words.

eye	gin	
be	lid ⟶	eyelid
log	pin	
un	in	
arm	bit	
rab	pit	

►Cut and glue words to finish the sentence.

is the colour of my teeth.

is the colour of a lab pup.

has no colour.

is a colour and a fruit.

is a colour and a candy.

is the colour of a sun-rise.

►Use a crayon to colour the words.

Black Lemon Yellow Mint Pink White

▶ Help the ant find his home.

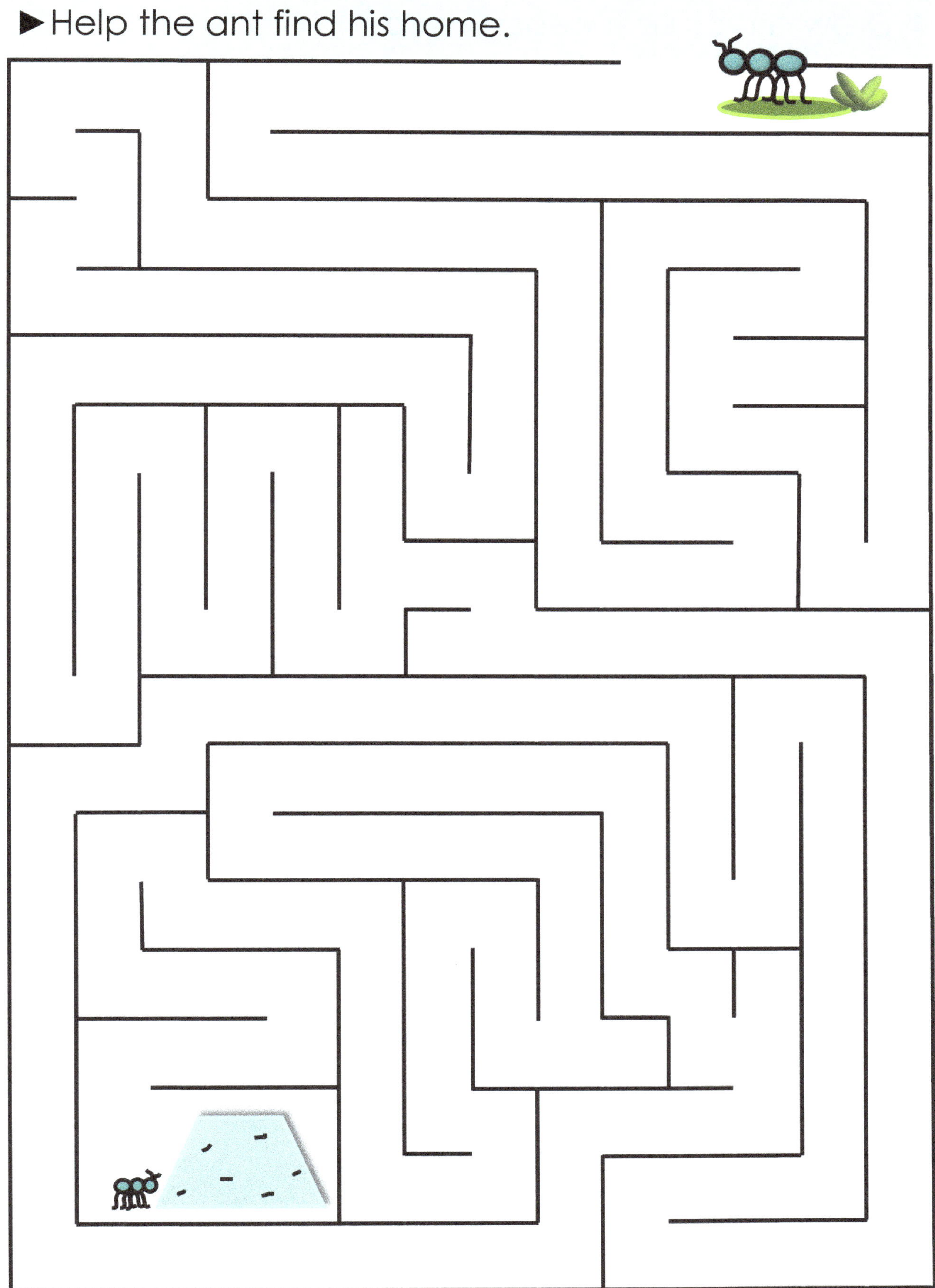

©FayeClunies-Ross

Creative Reading And Writing Book 3A

► Draw a picture for each word.

Sid

lid

kid

hid

► Read the story. Check a box.

Sid's Pig

Sid has a pet pig.

Sid has a big pet pig.

The pig likes to dig.

The pig likes to eat.

Sid will feed his big pet pig.

Sid is just a kid with a big pet pig.

► What rhymes?

bid

► Write a story. Draw a picture of your story.

I Like To Play

One day...

____

____

____

____

____

____

► Read and rewrite new words.

nose			
ears			
tail			

►Fill the sunflower with words you know.

►How many shapes can you find?

►Colour the picture.

©FayeClunies-Ross

► What is your last name? _______________________________

Home

1	2	3
4	5	6
7	8	9
*	0	#

► What is your phone number?

____ ____ ____ - ____ ____ ____ ____

► What is your address?

____

____

____

► Finish the sentence.

My   home   is

► Match to make new words.

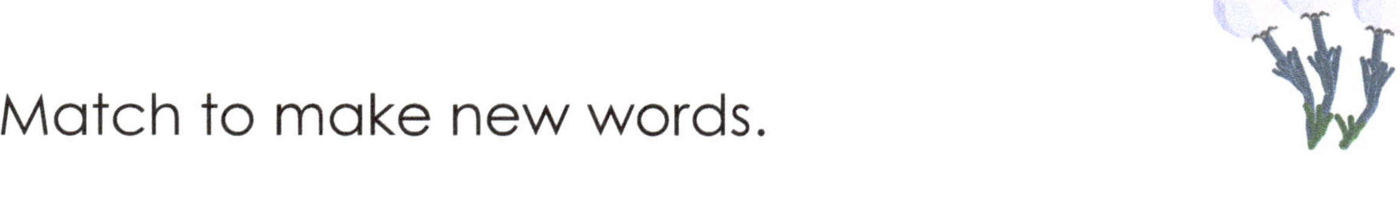

rab	mill	eye	gin
in	bit	be	lid
arm	to	log	pin
wind	pit	un	in
lip	up	rib	gan
pin	stick	be	bon

P U Z Z L E

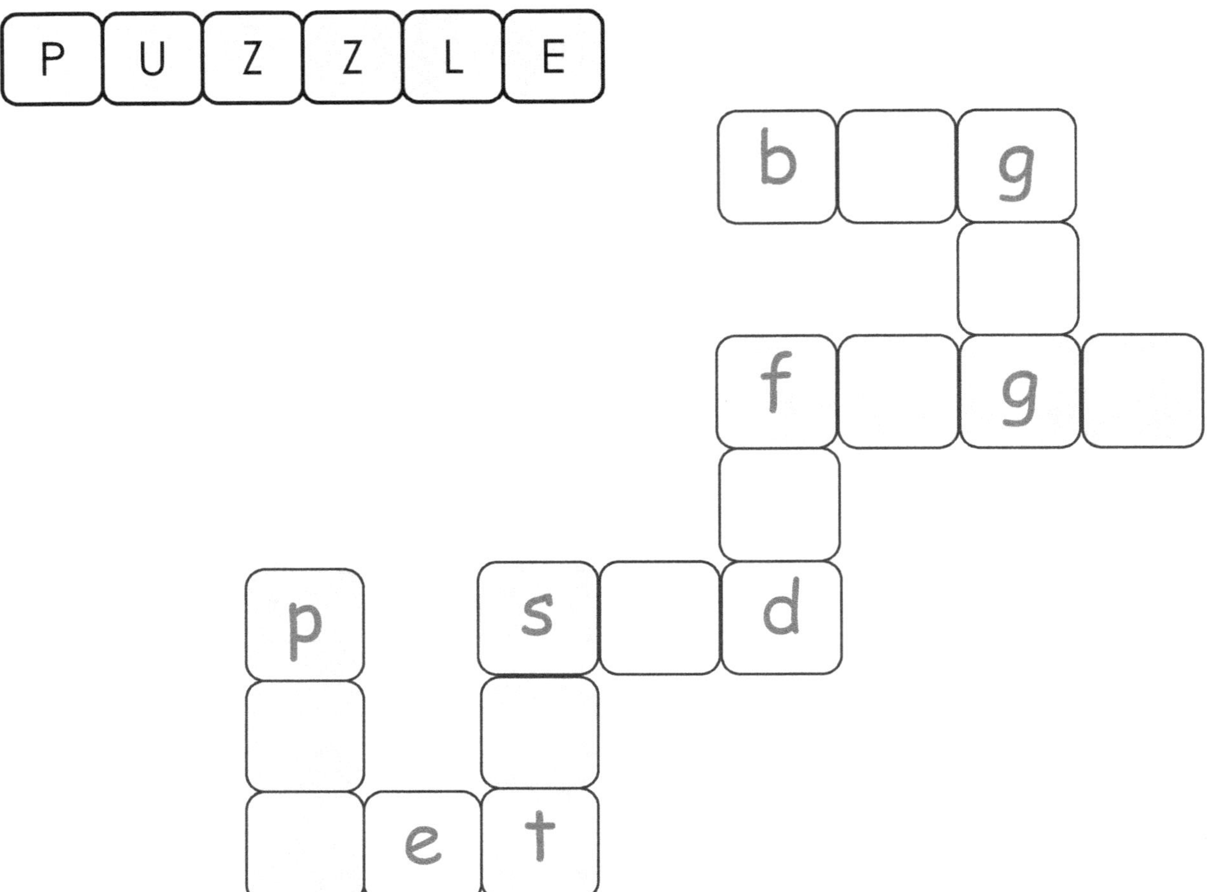

Clues.

Sid has a pet ____ ____ ____.

The pig is ____ ____ ____ .

The big pig likes to ____ ____ ____ in the mud.

The big pig likes to eat ____ ____ ____ ____.

▶Write other words. _______________________________

_______________________ _______________________ _______________________

▶Draw a picture of the story.

This is Sid.

Sid has a pet pig.

The pig likes to hide in
the tall grass.

The pig likes to hide in
the red barn.

The pig will say,

"Oink oink".

Sid will find that big
pink pig!

►Cut and glue words to finish the sentence.

A [ ] is a baby cat.

A [ ] is a baby chicken.

A [ ] is a baby pig.

A [ ] is a baby sheep.

A [ ] is a baby dog.

A [ ] is a baby goat.

| kid | lamb | chick | pup | piglet | kitten |

Help the pig find his friend.

► Draw a picture for each word.

pin

bin

fin

tin

► Read the story. Check a box.

Ted's Hen

Ted has a pet hen.
Ted has a nice pet hen.
The hen will win a rib-bon.
The hen will win a yellow ribbon.
Ted likes his hen.
Ted likes his good pet hen.

► What rhymes?

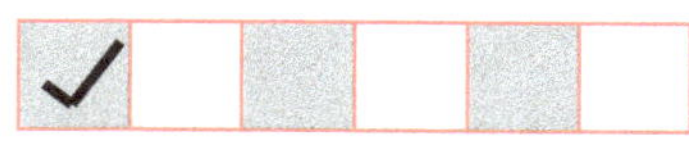

► Write a story. Draw a picture of your story.

<u>I Like to Win</u>

One day...

____

____

____

____

____

____

► Read and rewrite new words.

good			
ribbon			
that			

► Fill the dan-de-lions with words you know.

► Match.

id	will
in	pig
ill	tin
ig	sit
it	Sid
im	dim

► Match words.

what	who
where	what
why	when
when	where
how	why
who	how

► Read the sentences.

▶Unscramble the words.

 n i m t _______

 c p u _____

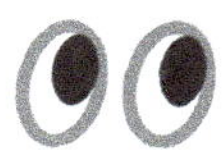 p n i k _______

 e e y s ______

 u n s ____

 d g o ____

▶Write the missing words.

The ___ ___ ___ had his ___ ___ ___ ___

on my ___ ___ ___ of ___ ___ ___

tea.

► Fill in the missing letters.

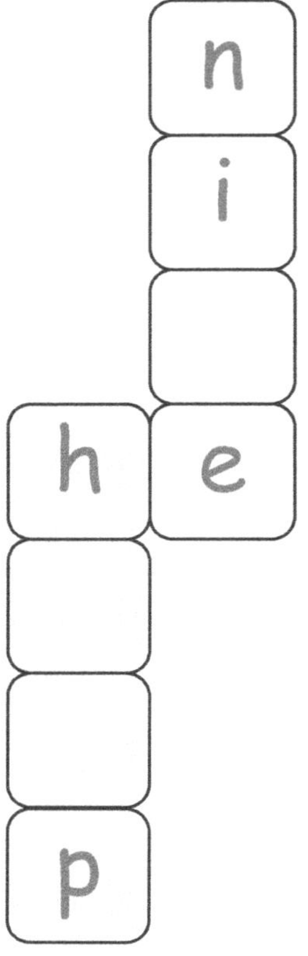

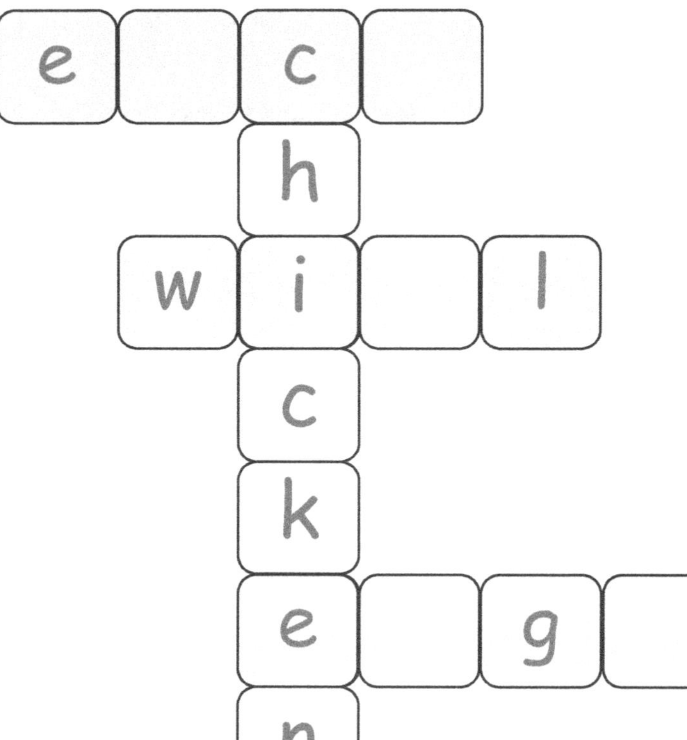

Clues.

Ted's hen ____ ____ ____ ____ win a ribbon.

Ted's hen is a ____ ____ ____ ____ red hen.

Ted's hen lays ____ ____ ____ ____ .

Ted's hen will lay an egg ____ ____ ____ ____ day.

Ben likes to ____ ____ ____ ____ find the eggs.

► Other word ________________________________

▶Draw a picture of the story.

This is Ted's hen.

The hen likes to run in
the tall grass.

The hen likes to eat
seeds.

The hen likes to dr-ink
from a dish.

The hen likes to eat in
the gar-den!

"Shoo, shoo," says Ted,
"out of the garden!"

►Cut and glue words to finish the sentence.

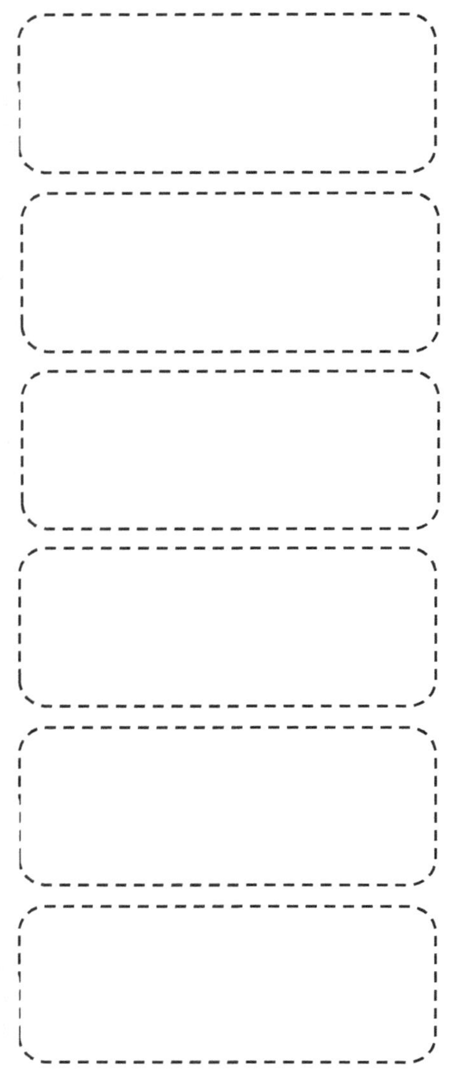

Who has a pet pig?

The big pig is ...

Sid is just a...

Sid's pig likes to eat...

Sid lives on a...

Pigs live in a...

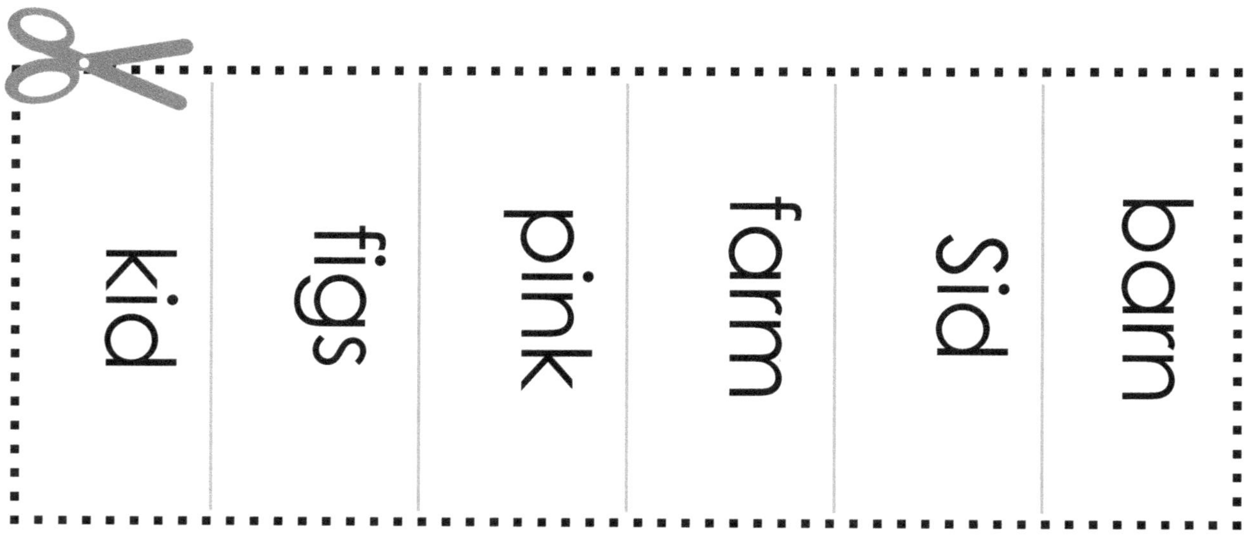

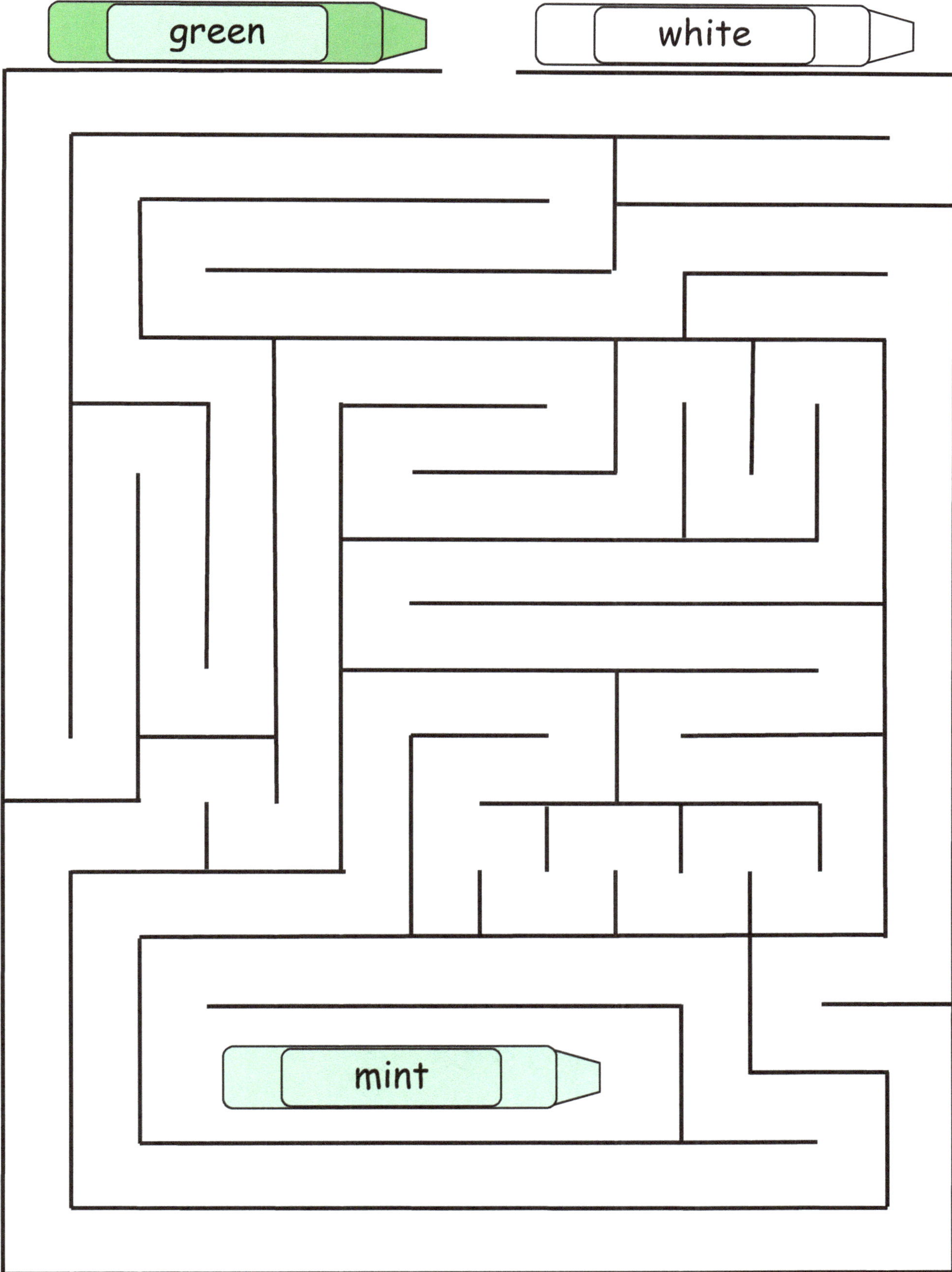

©FayeClunies-Ross

Creative Reading And Writing Book 3A

►Draw a picture for each word.

bit

mitt

pit

zit

►Read the story. Check a box.

Little Rabbit

Mit-tens is a little rab-bit.
Mittens is a wee little rabbit.
Mittens likes to run and kick.
Mittens likes to sn-iff and skip.
If I had a wee little rabbit,
I would love it!

►What rhymes?

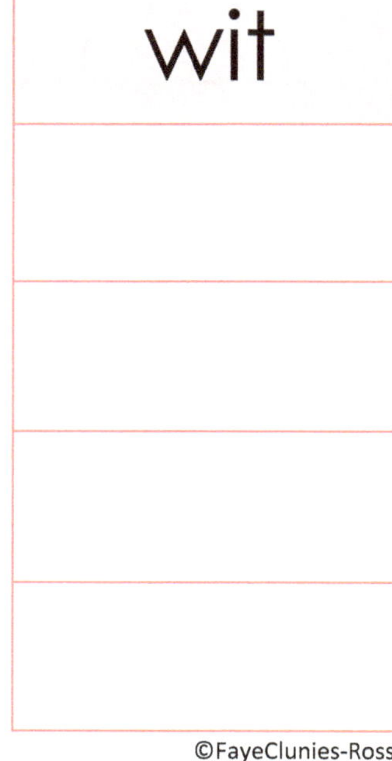

My Little Rabbit

Once upon a

time...

would			
hide			
barn			

▶ Write the words you know on the box.

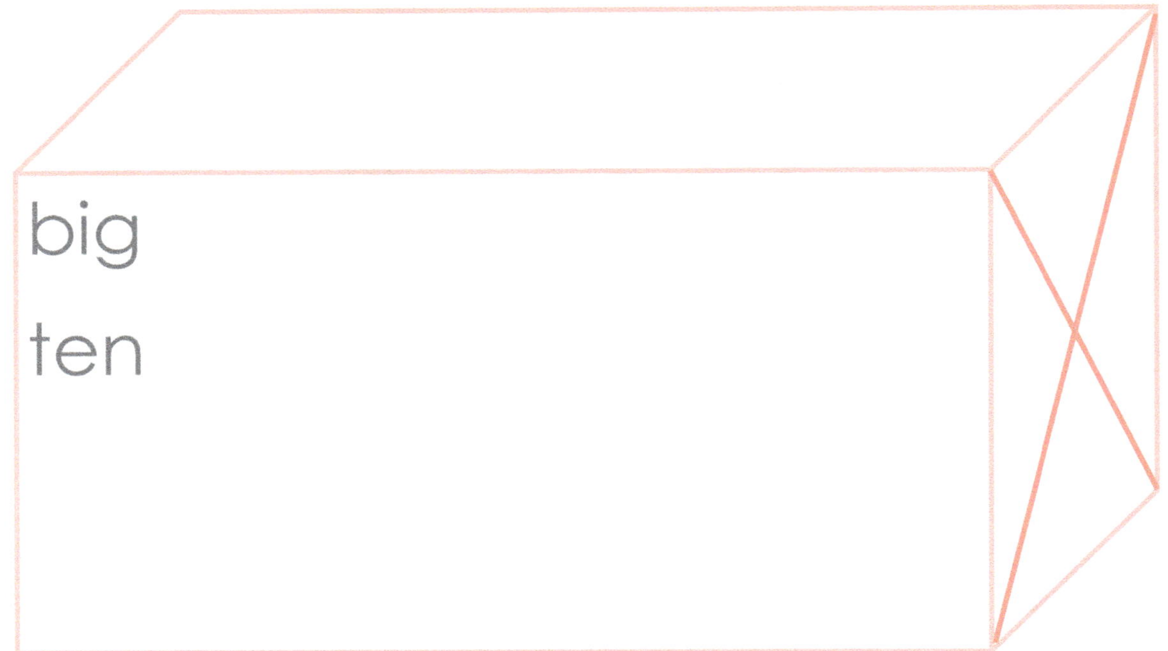

▶ Draw a fig...

▶ Finish the sentence.

The   big   box

► Match.

ill	pin
ig	will
it	Sid
im	sit
in	big
id	him

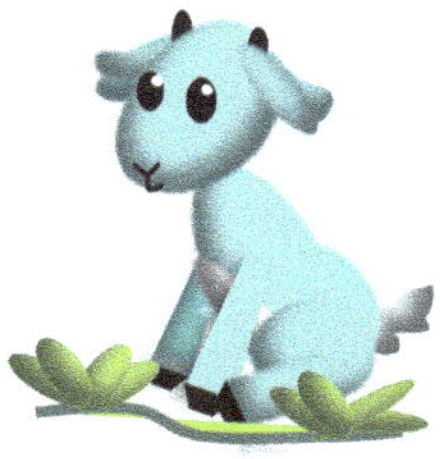

► What rhymes?

in

► Circle the vowels. Write how many.

Horse Paddock	
Hay loft	
Cattle guard	

► Match.

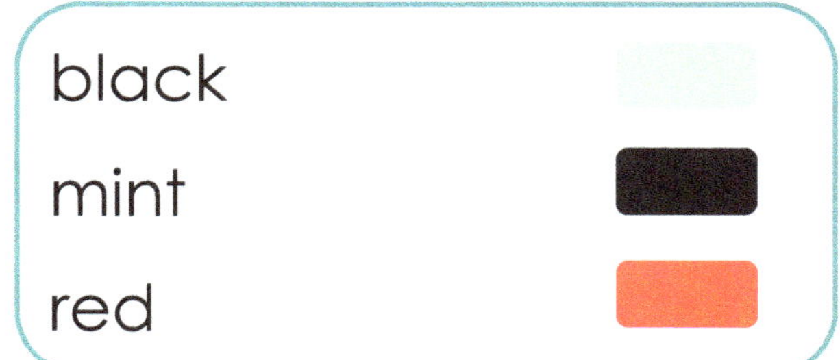

► Finish the sentence with a colour word.

The ________ goat likes to

eat   wet   hay.

♥ How to Draw a Rabbit ♥

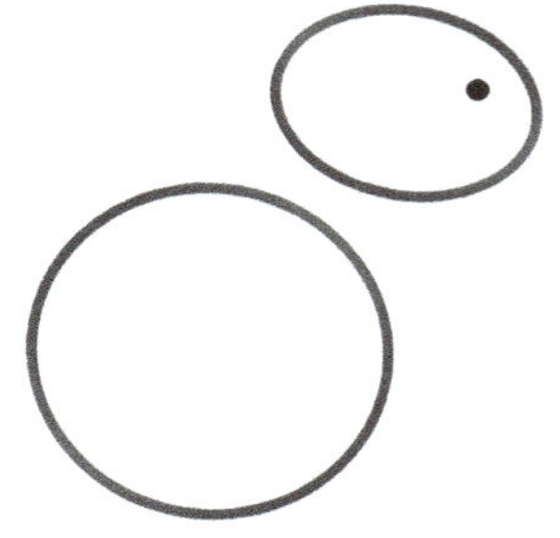

body and head

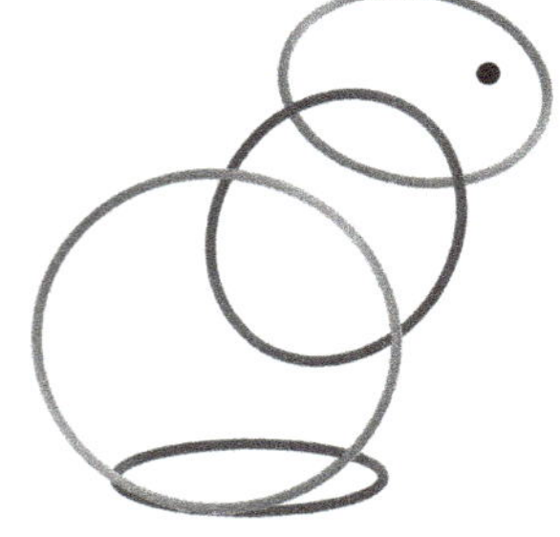

neck and foot

tail and toe

ears and mouth

colour

shade

▶ Draw a rabbit.

▶ What would you name a pet rabbit?

____

▶ Match and write new words.

pig	up	
rip	pen ⟶	pigpen
lip	bon	
pin	off	
rib	mill	
wind	stick	

♫ One little, two little, three little chickadees,

Four little, five little, six little chickadees, ♪

♫ Seven little, eight little, nine little chickadees,

All in a row for a meal, peep, peep, peep, peep. ♪

▶ Write the number words.

one	two	

▶ Cut out and fold to make finger puppets.

Cut along the dotted line. Fold on the solid line. Glue or tape puppet to the end of a popsicle stick.
Use as a pointer stick while reading.

► What colour does pink and white make?

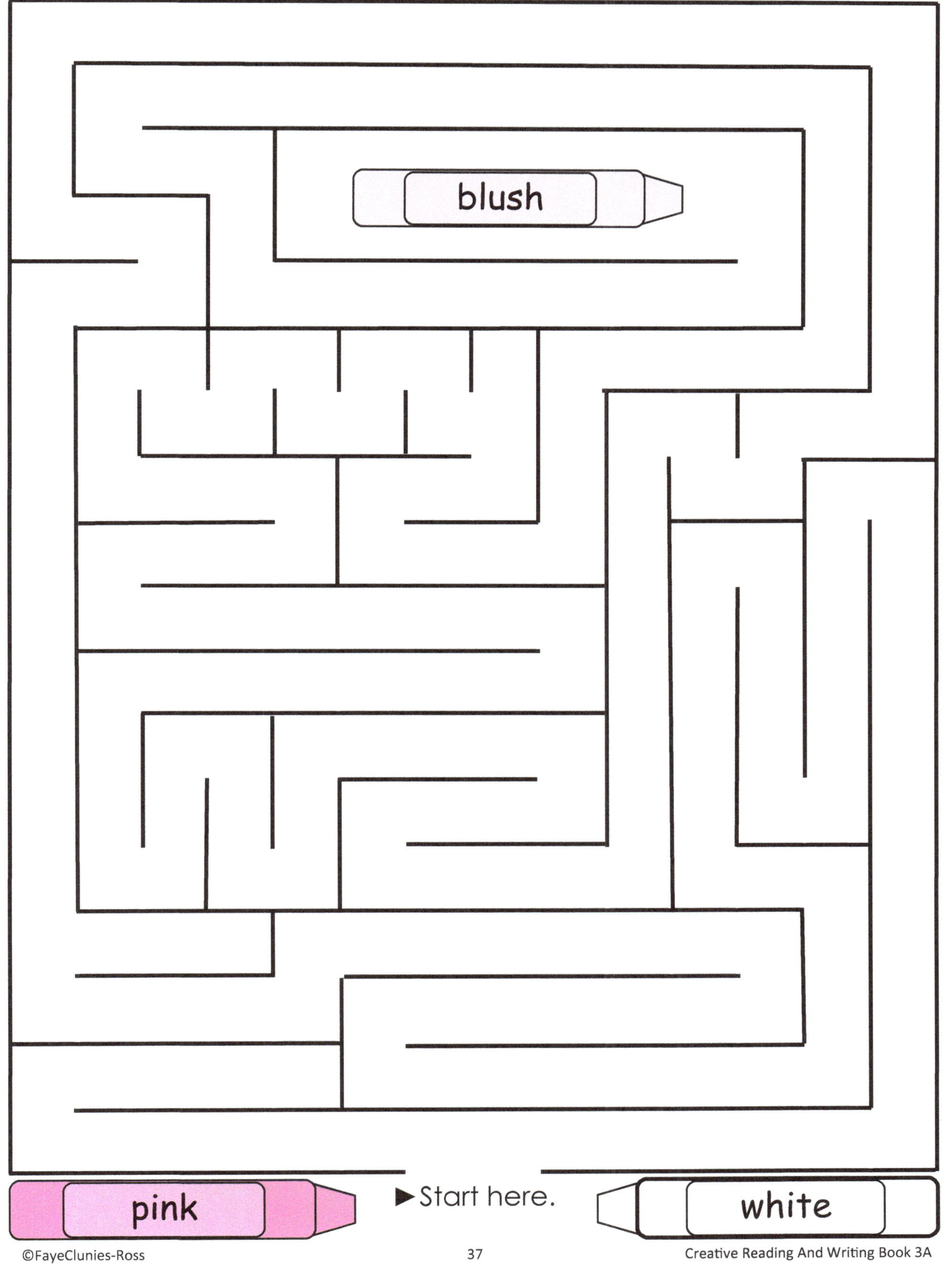

► Draw a picture for each word.

bill

quill

mill

ill

► Read the story. Check a box.

Papa

Papa works on the farm.

Papa works at the mill.

He will work hard on the farm.

He will work hard at the mill.

Papa is glad he can work.

Papa is glad he can pay the bills.

► What rhymes?

▶ Write a story. Draw a picture of your story.

<u>At The Flour Mill</u>

Everyday...

____

____

____

____

____

____

▶ Read and rewrite new words.

work			
hard			
pay			

▶Fill the cloud with words you know.

▶How many shapes can you find? Colour the picture.

▶Write a sentence.

► Match words.

write   colour

read   circle

match   read

finish   write

circle   match

colour   finish

► What rhymes?

pig

► Circle the vowels. Write how many.

Pig Farm	
Hog Barn	

► Match.

black	
green	
mint	

red	
pink	
white	

► Finish the sentence with a colour word.

The   pig   likes   to   sit

on   the   grass.

▶Fill in the missing letters.

P U Z Z L E

f a m i l _

P _ p _

m _ _ l

r y

w _ _ k s

Clues.

___ ___ ___ ___ is a farmer.

Papa will grow ___ ___ ___ and oats.

Papa ___ ___ ___ ___ ___ at the mill too.

The mill is a flour ___ ___ ___ ___.

Papa works hard for his ___ ___ ___ ___ ___ ___.

▶Other word ________________

► Draw a picture of the story.

Papa works at the mill.

Mama works in the garden.

Mom works at the bank.

Dad works at the store.

I work at school.

My family will work and help each other!

♫ One little, two little, three little chickadees.

Four little, five little, six little chickadees, ♪

♫ Seven little, eight little, nine little chickadees,

All in a row for a meal, peep, peep, peep, peep. ♪

► Write the number words.

one		

► Cut and fold to make finger puppets.

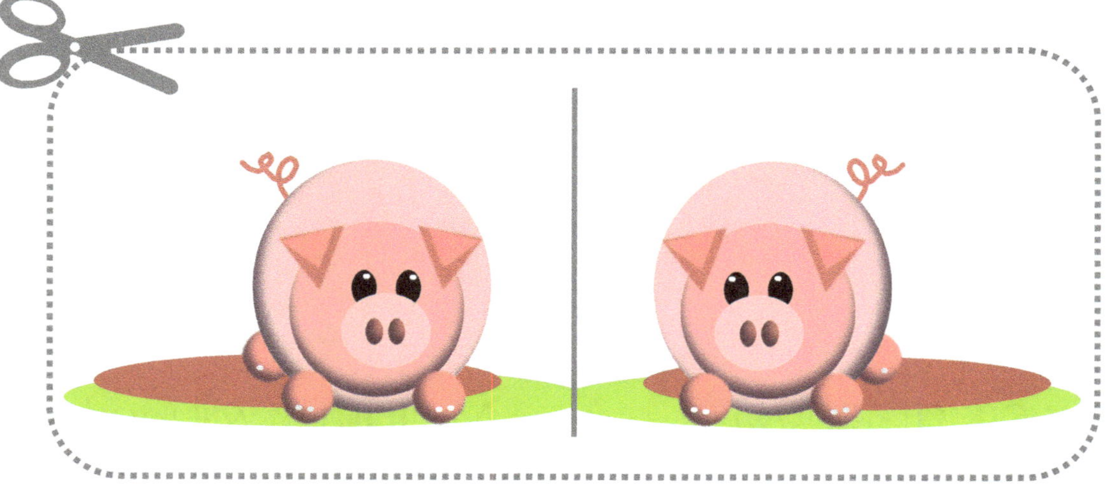

Cut along the dotted line. Fold on the solid line. Glue or tape puppet to the end of a popsicle stick. Use as a pointer stick while reading.

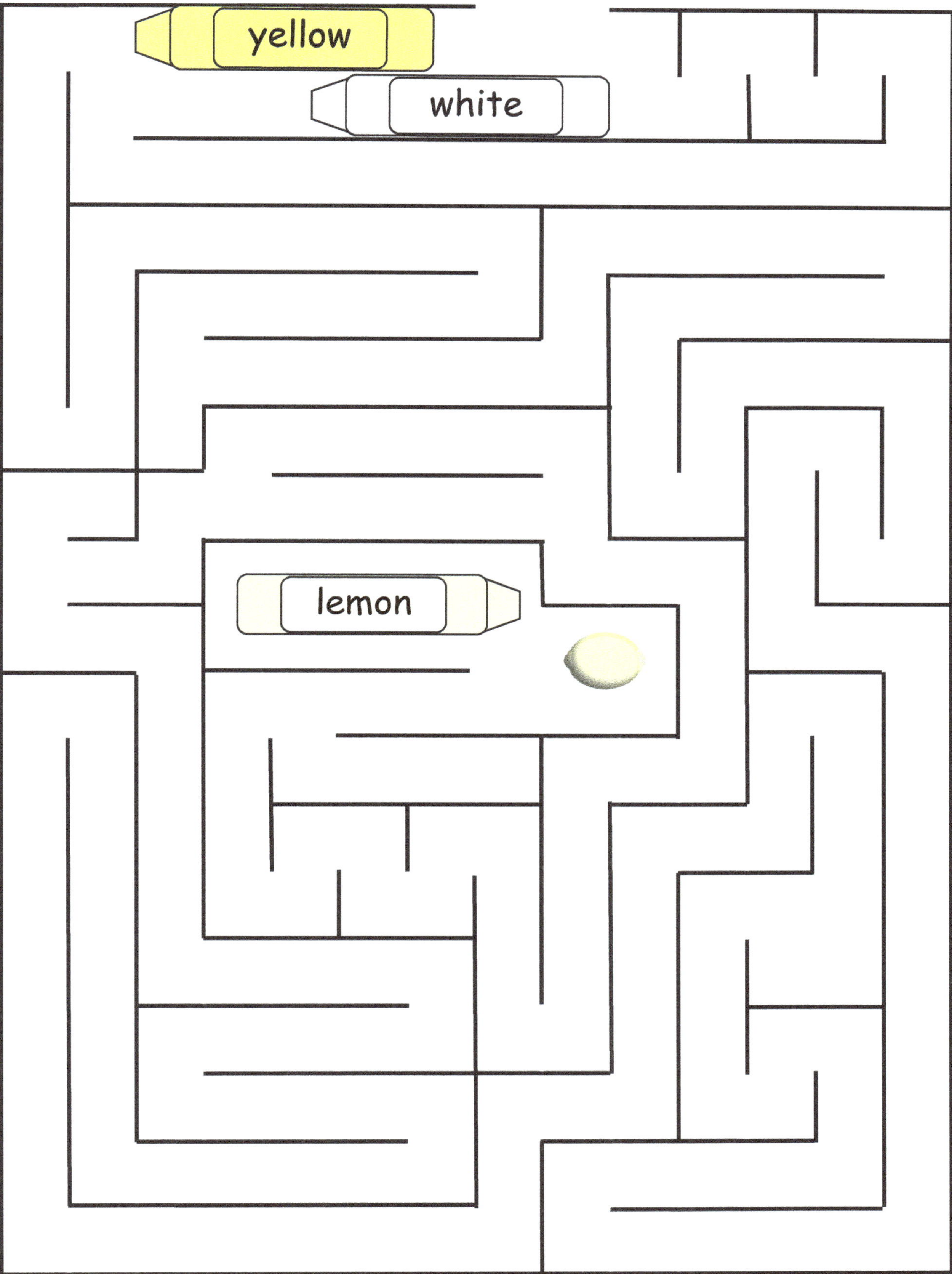
yellow
white
lemon

►Draw a picture for each word.

zip-line

lip-stick

tip-toe

hip-po

►Read the story. Check a box.

Tea Time

Mama likes tea time.
Papa likes tea time.
Mama will sip her tea.
Papa will sip his tea too.
Finn will see. Finn will tiptoe in.
"Come have tea," said Mama.
Finn will sit and sip tea too.

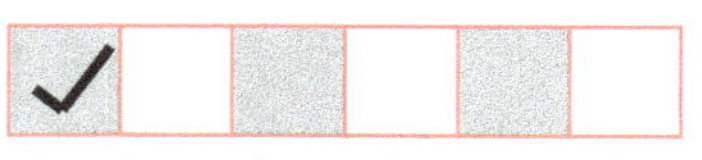

►What rhymes?

sip

►Write a story. Draw a picture of your story.

<u>The Zip-Line</u>

One day...

____

____

____

____

____

►Read and rewrite new words.

tea			
time			
line			

▶ Write the words you know on the leaves.

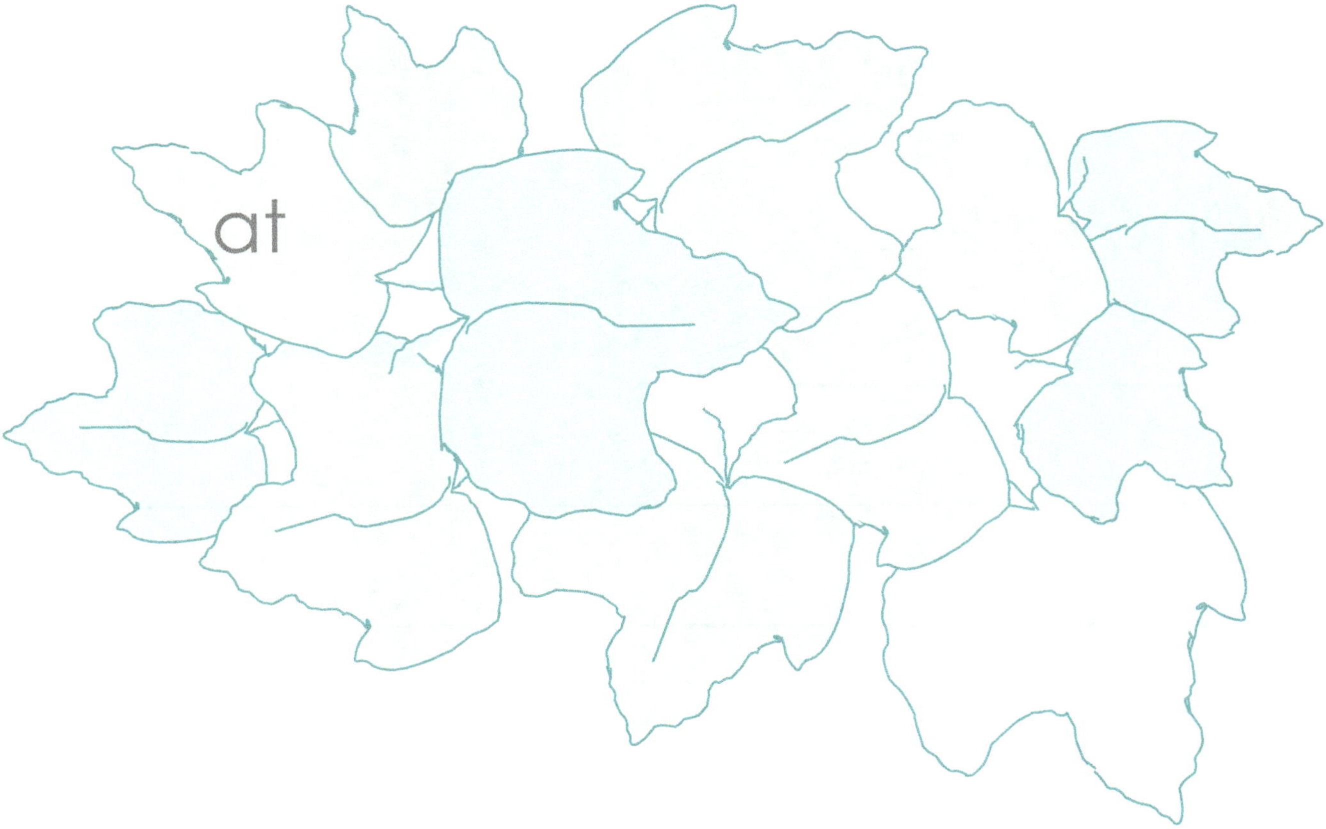

at

▶ Write a sentence.

▶ Draw leaves...

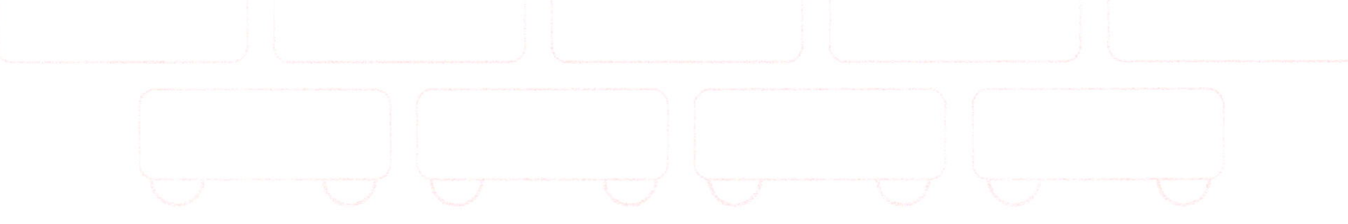

| **under** | **in** | **by** |
| the lamb. | the barn. | the tree. |

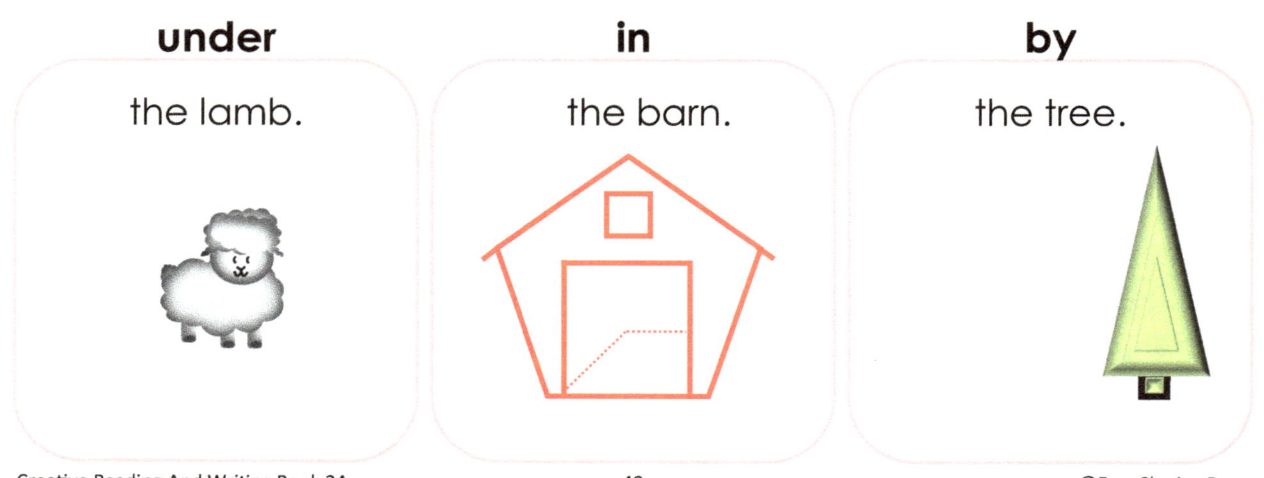

► Match words.

what	who
where	how
how	when
when	what
why	why
who	where

► What rhymes?

ill

► Circle the vowels. Write how many.

Milk parlor	
Feed truck	
Livestock	

► Match.

black	
mint	
red	

green	
pink	
white	

► Finish the sentence.

What   a   cute   lamb!

So   soft   and

 Ii

says ĭ, as in cinnamon

says ĭ, as in indigo 

▶ What colour is it? 

▶ What colour is it? 

▶ Finish the sentence.

Mom	made	a		tea.

	It	was	so	good.

▶ Match.

▶ Write the colour.

mint 

indigo 

cinnamon 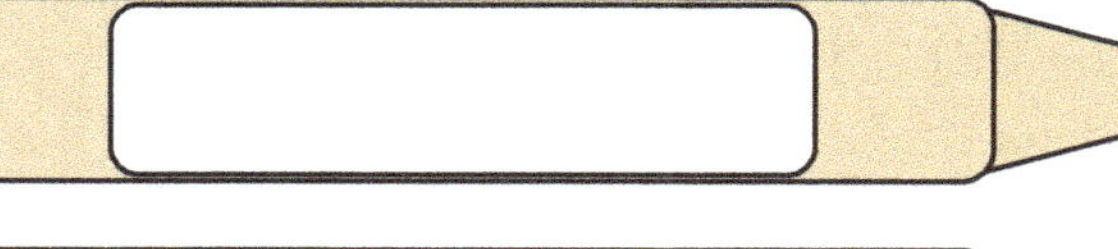

tan

green

▶Write a letter.

Dear

____

____

____

____

____

From,

____

▶Finish the sentence with a colour word.

The   rabbit   likes   to

sit   by   the   pond.

▶Draw an ant... 

in   **on**   **by**

a flower.   a flower.   some flowers.

▶ Unscramble the words.

 n a t _____ _____ _____

 f g i _____ _____ _____

 e r d _____ _____ _____

 l e w l _____ _____ _____ _____

 b l a m _____ _____ _____ _____

 e e r t _____ _____ _____ _____

▶ Write the missing words.

The ___ ___ ___ ___ and the ___ ___ ___ are

looking under the fig ___ ___ ___ ___

for a good ___ ___ ___ to eat.

©FayeClunies-Ross

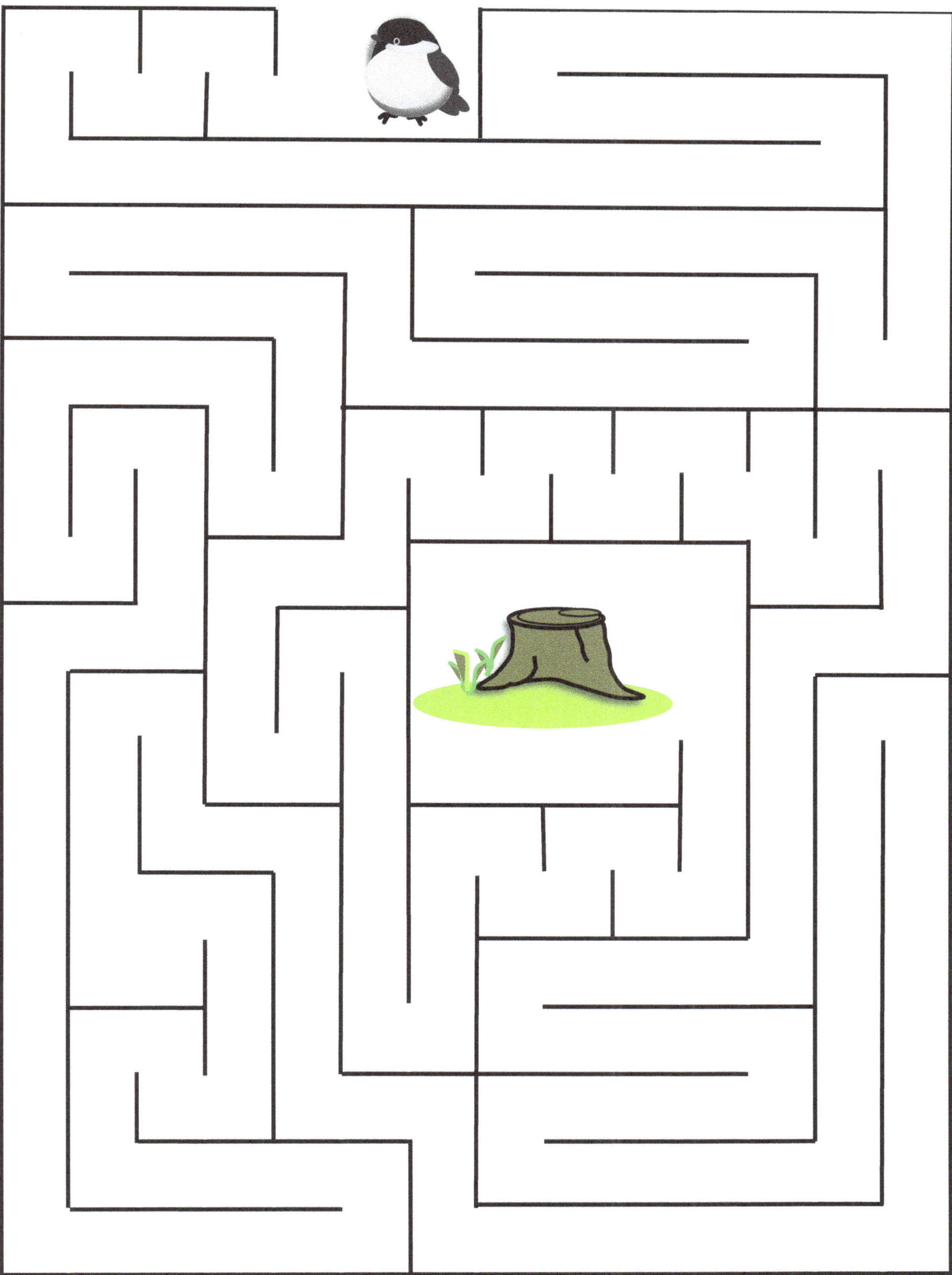

▶ Draw a picture for each word.

bib

crib

rib

sib-ling

▶ Read the story. Check a box.

New Baby

Ben has a new baby sis.

Tess is Ben's sister.

Tess will cry. Ben will help.

Tess needs a bib. Ben will help.

Tess needs her crib. Ben will help.

Ben and Tess are sib-lings.

Ben loves his new baby sis-ter!

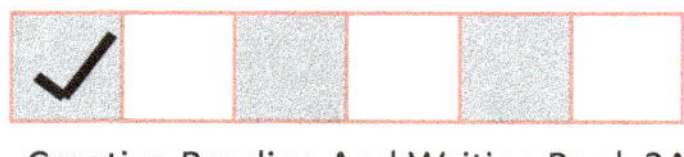

▶ What rhymes?

nib

► Write a story. Draw a picture of your story.

<u>A Day at the Park</u>

One day...

____

____

____

____

____

____

► Read and rewrite new words.

sister			
baby			
needs			

► Write the words you know on the fig tree.

fig

► Write a sentence.

► Draw a fig tree...

on

a hill.

by

a pond.

in

a garden.

► Read and cross out 3-in-a-row, tic tac toe!

be	my	to
on	me	at
in	of	as

Example

and	by	the
so	to	is
be	on	or

me	ex	ok
do	it	by
he	we	if

► Draw an ant ...

on

a stump.

under

a dry twig

by

the tin can.

► Match.

pink

mint

blush

emerald

green

► Write the colour.

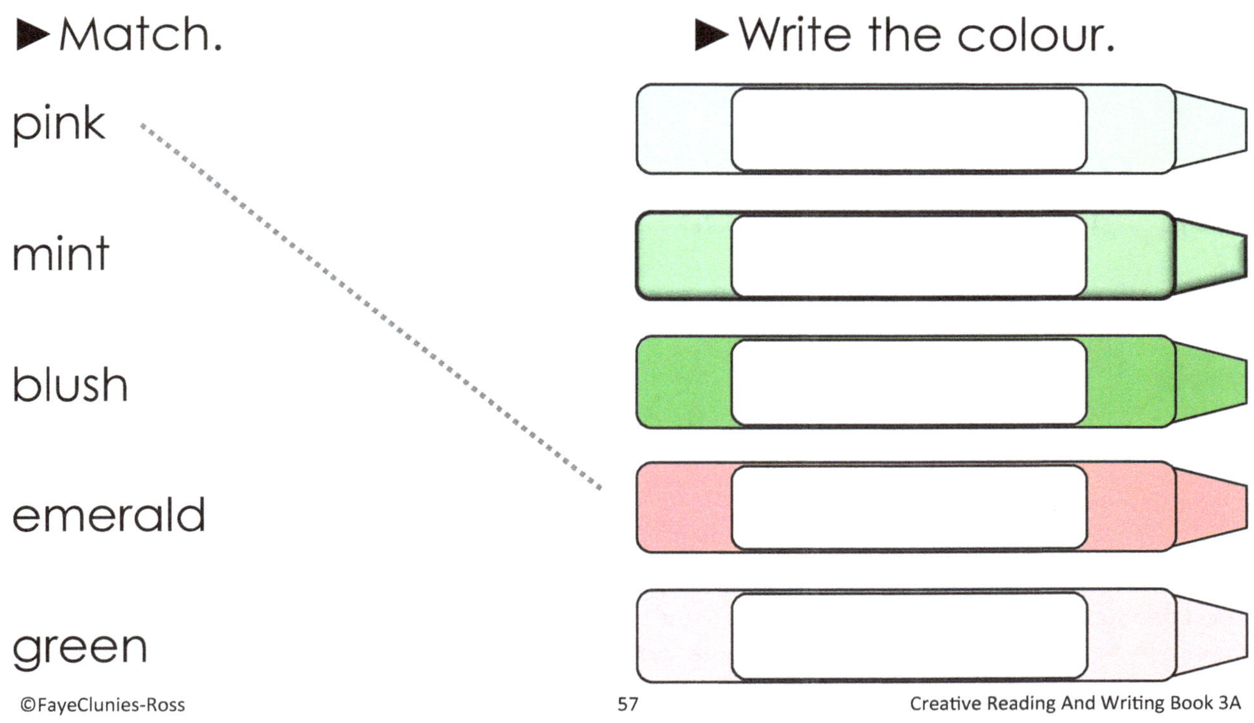

► Read and cross out 5-in-a-row on the Game Cards.

bid	hid	kid	lid	Sid	big	dig	fig
pig	wig	bill	fill	ill	mill	pill	till
bin	fin	pin	tin	win	hip	lip	rip
sip	zip	bit	mitt	pit	sit	wit	dim

► Write how many.

	cinnamon		mint		indigo
	pink		green		

Let's Play!

Game Card 1				
bid	wig	pin	mitt	big
pill	rip	pig	fin	bit
Sid	mill	☆	lip	it
dim	zip	fig	hid	bill
tin	pit	dig	till	sip

Game Card 2				
sip	lid	ill	hip	wit
kid	fill	win	sit	dig
fill	big	☆	pill	rip
hid	bill	tin	pit	pig
fin	bit	bin	zip	dim

Read one word at a time from the list above. Cross out the word on each game card. The first card to make 5-in-a-row wins! **Option** for a longer game; play cards until there are TWO five-in-a –row.

The pig says, oink.

The lamb says, baa.

The hen says, cluck.

The cat says, meow.

The farm has a lot of animals.

The animals live in the big red barn.

►Cut and glue words to finish the sentence.

_________ is your name?

_________ do you live?

_________ is your birthday?

_________ old are you?

_________ do you like candy?

_________ is your best friend?

Who What Where When Why How

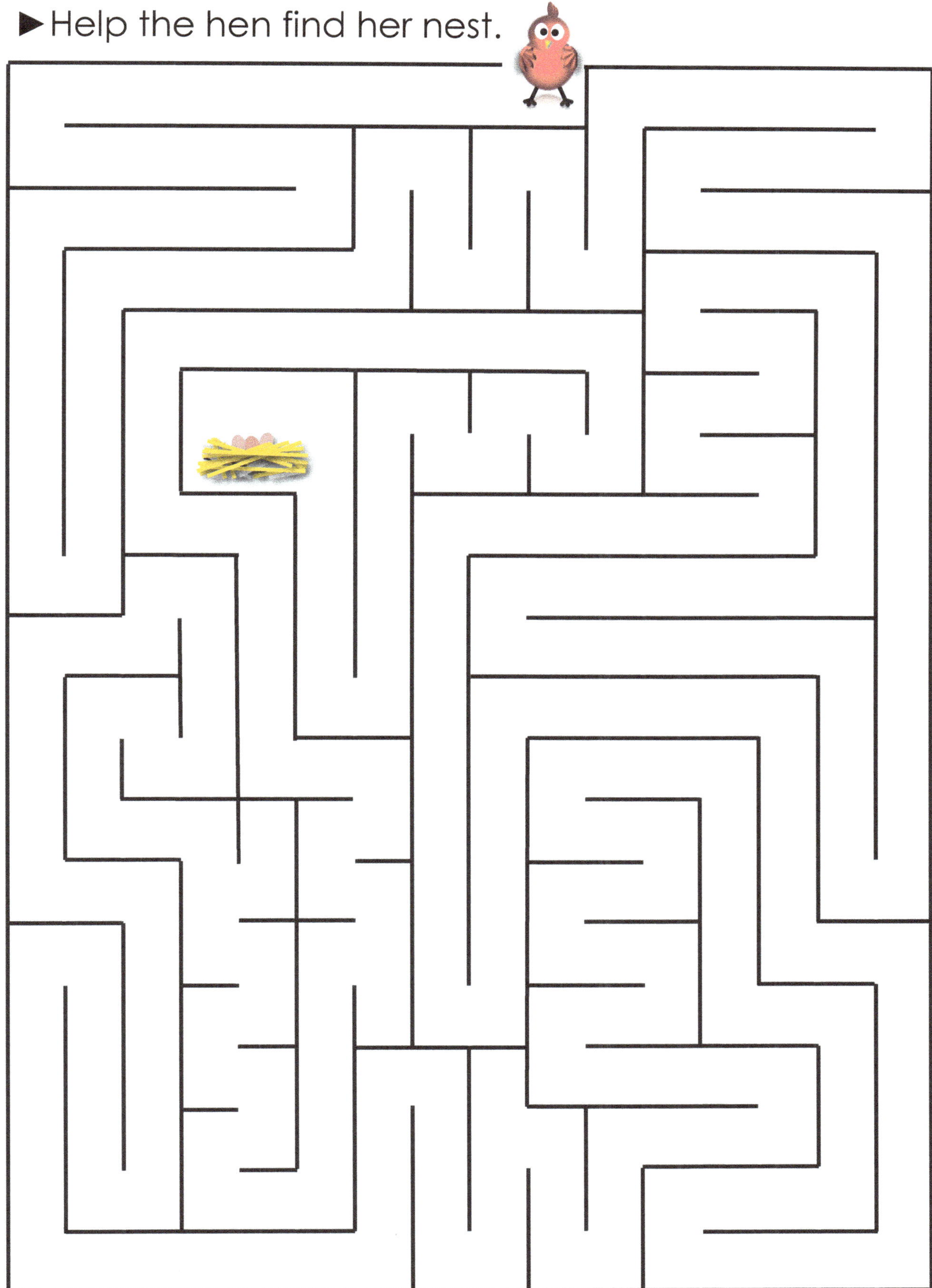

► Draw a picture for each word.

limb

Tim

rim

Jim

► Read the story. Check a box.

Tim and Jim

Tim likes to fish.

Jim likes to fish.

Tim likes to fish for bass.

Jim likes to fish for cod.

Tim and Jim like to go fish-ing.

They like to go fishing at the pond.

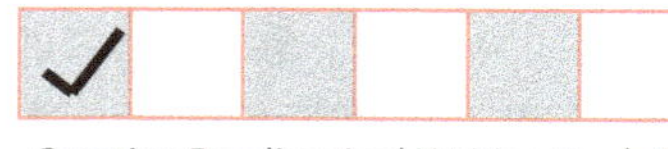

► What rhymes?

dim

► Write a story. Draw a picture of your story.

<u>A Day at the Pond</u>

One day...

____

____

____

____

____

____

► Read and rewrite new words.

fish			
pond			
they			

► Match words.   ► What rhymes?

limb	him
whim	Jim
him	dim
dim	whim
Jim	limb
rim	Tim
Tim	rim

rim

► Write the missing words.

him   Jim   limb   Tim   whim

___ ___ ___ loves to fish.

___ ___ ___ loves to fish with ___ ___ ___ too.

Tim and Jim will go fishing on a ___ ___ ___ ___ .

They will put the fish on a will-ow ___ ___ ___ ___.

►Finish the sentence with a colour word.

A   hen   ran   around

the   big   barn.

►Draw a pond...

by   **near**   **under**

a hill.   the barn.   a tree.

►Write the vowels on the blocks.

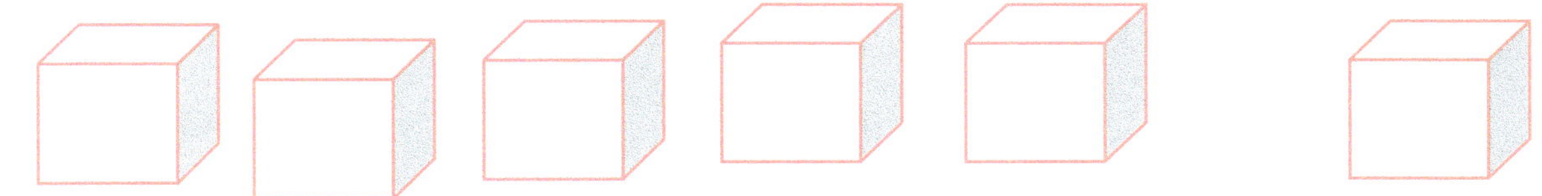

►Match sounds.

		id	sin
a	nut	ig	lid
e	cat	in	wig
i	ton	ill	mitt
o	pen	it	mill
u	bin	ib	rib

▶ Write a letter.

Dear

____

____

____

____

From,

▶ Draw a wig...

on	**on**	**on**
a pig.	rabbit.	a goat.

▶ Finish the sentence.

The   rabbit   found

Tim is at the pond.

Tim will ca-tch two fish.

Jim is at the pond.

Jim will catch one fish.

Mom will fry the fish.

Tim and Jim sure like
fri-ed fish!

►Fill in the missing letters.

| P | U | Z | Z | L | E |

f _ s h   l _ _ v _

f _ s h _ _ g   p

_ _ _ i _ _

f _ y   b a r n

Clues.

Jim went fishing down at the ___ ___ ___ ___.

Tim went ___ ___ ___ ___ ___ ___ ___ too.

Jim and Tim will get two ___ ___ ___ ___ each.

Mom will ___ ___ ___ the fish for dinner.

Jim and Tim ___ ___ ___ ___ fishing!

►Write other words _____________ _____________

_____________ _____________

► Read and race to the top! Play 4-in-a-row.

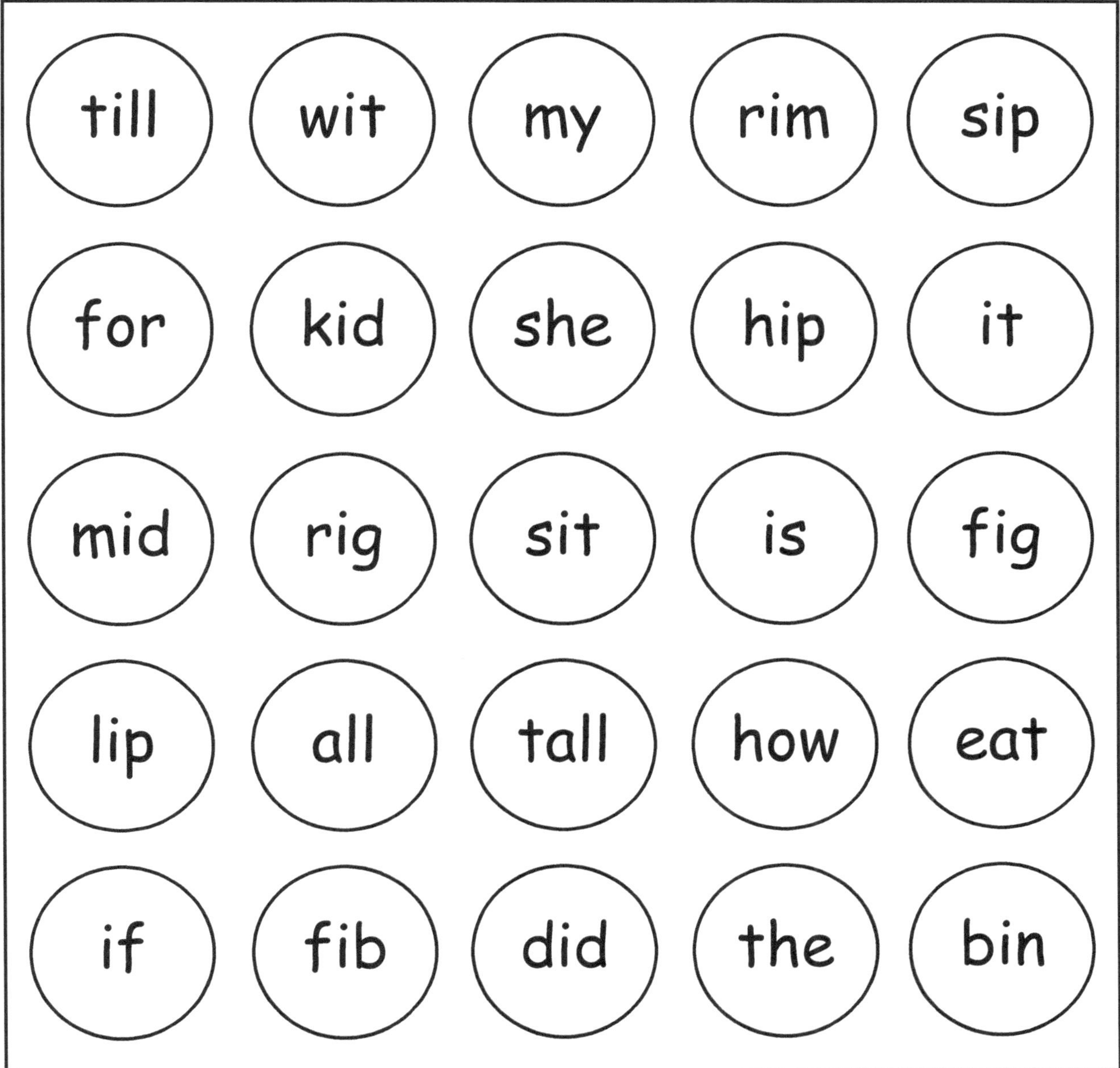

Start at the bottom. Use 2 different coloured crayons (to play once) or 2 different coloured paper (to play more than once). Take turns reading and colouring in a circle. The first player to make 4 in a row wins!

► Write a sentence with the winning words.

I = y

y says, **i,** as in sky

sky blue

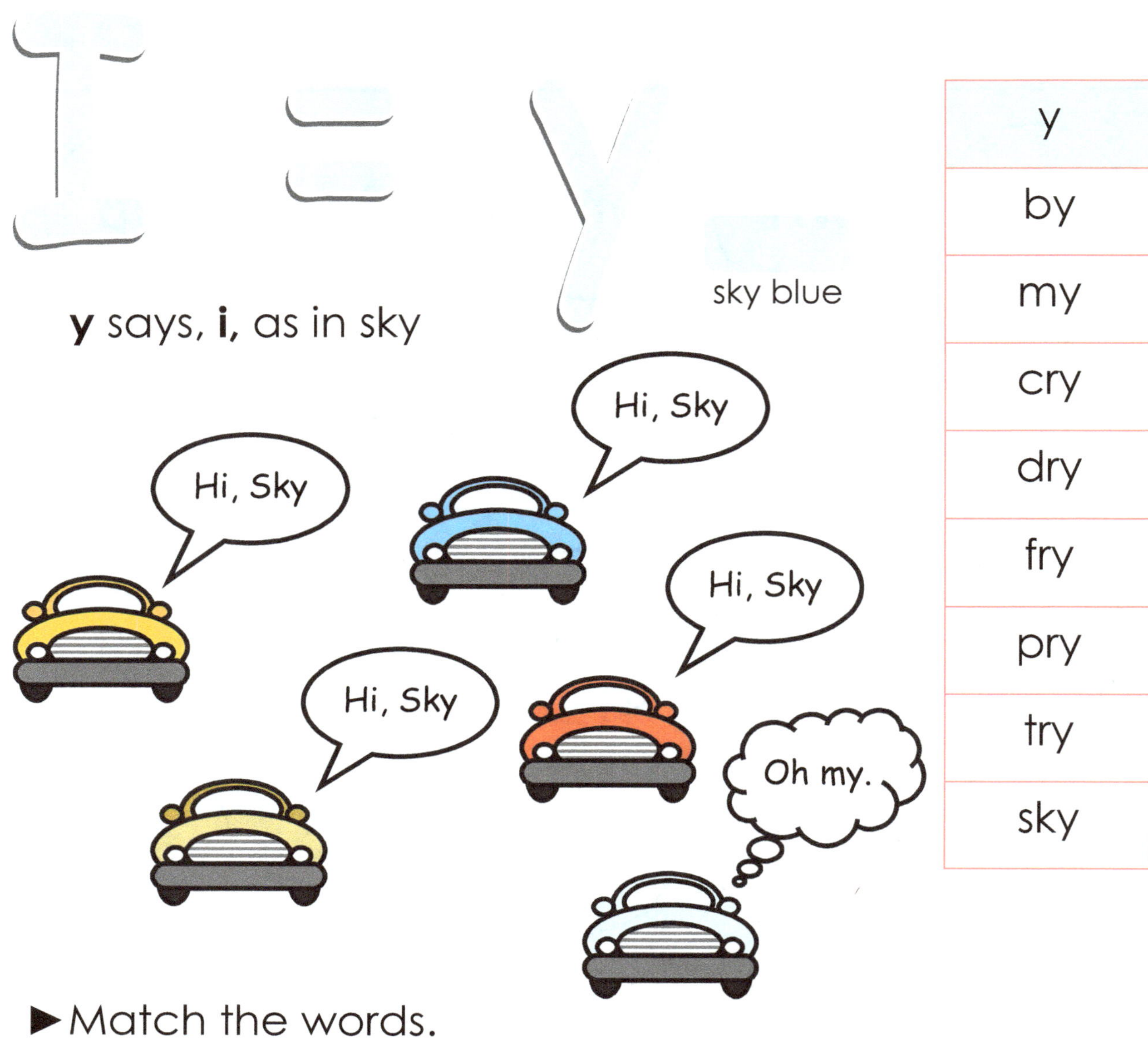

y
by
my
cry
dry
fry
pry
try
sky

►Match the words.

by	my	fry	dry
my	try	cry	fry
dry	by	dry	cry
fry	sky	my	pry
try	dry	by	by
sky	fry	pry	my

► What rhymes? ► Write what happens next.

► Write the missing words.

my   by   cry   dry   try   Sky

I am Amber and this is ____ ____ sister Sky.

____ ____ ____ likes to draw and write.

Sky likes to draw with ____ ____ ____ ch-alk.

I will ____ ____ ____ to draw ____ ____ my-self.

I will not ____ ____ ____ if I make a mess.

► Match words.   ► Write words that are similar.

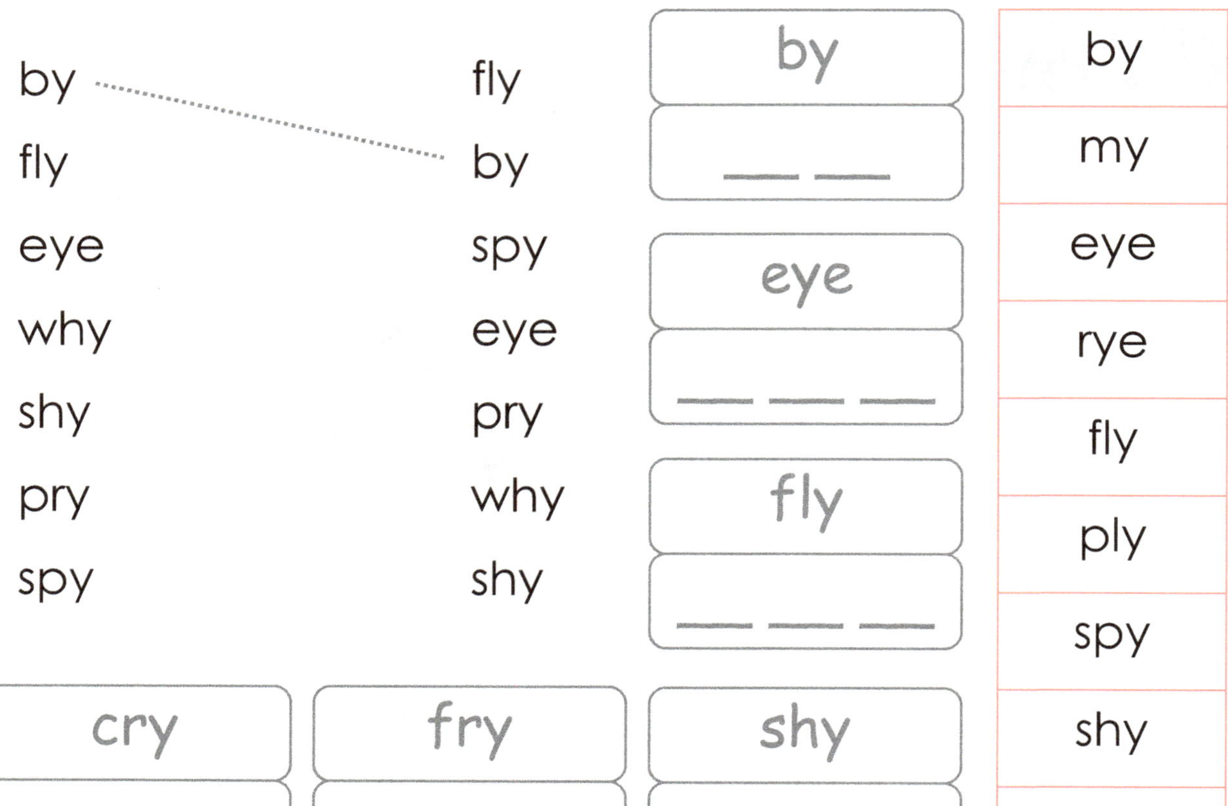

by	fly
fly	by
eye	spy
why	eye
shy	pry
pry	why
spy	shy

by
___ ___

eye
___ ___ ___ ___

fly
___ ___ ___ ___

cry
___ ___ ___ ___

fry
___ ___ ___ ___

shy
___ ___ ___ ___

by
my
eye
rye
fly
ply
spy
shy
why

► Circle the vowels. Write how many.

Fishing pond	
Grain feeder	
Water pump	

► Read the sentence.

That   cute   little   pig   lives

outside   in   a   pigsty.

► Write what happens next.   ► What rhymes?

► Match words.   ► Make compound words.

my	ply	by	self
shy	my	my	eyed
ply	shy	dry	pass
rye	why	ply	out
why	fly	try	line
fly	rye	sky	wood

►Read the sentence.

| Tim | and | Jim | will | try |

| to | fry | the | fish. |

►Match and write new words.

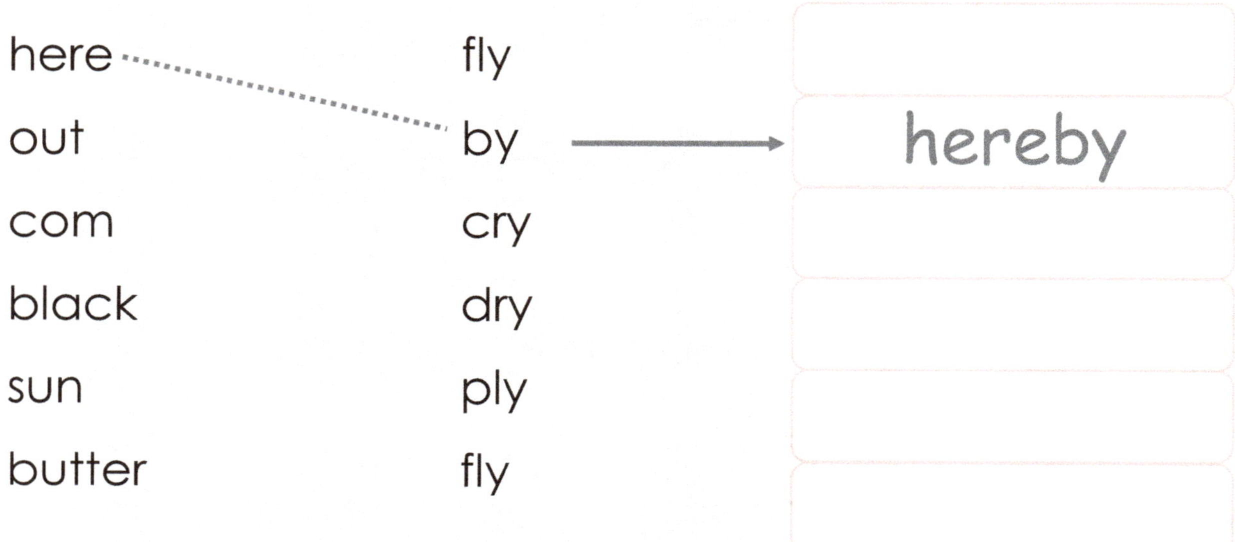

here	fly	
out	by	**hereby**
com	cry	
black	dry	
sun	ply	
butter	fly	

►Write the missing words.

shy   my   why   eye   spy

I ____ ____ ____ with my little eye, some-thing...

I spy with ____ ____ little eye, some-thing...

I spy with my little ____ ____ ____, something...

Tell me ____ ____ ____. Don't be ____ ____ ____.

►Draw a picture of your family story.

This is me.   This is my family.

This is my house.   This is my room.

This is my pet.   This is what I like to eat.

► Draw a picture of your favourite place to camp.

My favourite camping spot is _________________

____

_______________________________________.

► Read and match.

say	family	place	done
does	say	spot	place
your	your	picture	outside
lake	does	outside	picture
family	lake	done	spot

Quiz   Name ________________________________

►Read the words to your teacher.

mitt	sit	pit	bit	wit	fit	it	kid
hid	lid	bid	pin	bin	tin	fin	win
sin	big	pig	fig	dig	wig	till	will
pill	bill	mill	rip	lip	hip	zip	sip

►Write the words your teacher says.

►Write a sentence.

►Write the vowels...   ►and sometimes.

"I am thankful for ________________________________.

Are you ready for Book 4?

Just a few teaching tips!

►Practice the short vowel sounds until your child knows them well. Say the short sounds,

> ă, as in cat, ă… ă… ă.
>
> ĕ, as in hen, ĕ… ĕ… ĕ.
>
> ĭ, as in pig, ĭ… ĭ… ĭ.
>
> ŏ as in dog, ŏ… ŏ… ŏ.
>
> ŭ as in duck, ŭ… ŭ… ŭ.

►Before the child reads a story, review any unfamiliar words.

►As your child works through the book make a separate list of words that may need extra practice. Use this list for a spelling test.

►Another option for "Draw a picture of your story" is to print an online picture or cut and paste from a magazine.

►Play the memory game with letters, blends and words.

►Attach flashcards around the house then play "touch and say." The child simply finds the card, touches it and says the word 3 times.

►Hang a string and use clothespins to pin up flashcards.

►Reward your child often. Rewards can be as easy as drawing a smiley face on the work page or giving the child a small treat like raisins or chocolate chips for work completed.

►Use a star chart. Kids love stickers!

►Use a calendar to write a new spelling word for each day.

►Extra teacher directions are written throughout the book.

Enjoy!

Word List

2-letter words

ad, am, an, as, at, be, he, me, we, ye, hi, if, in, is, it, go, no, so, ok, do, to, of, on, or, up, ax, ex, ox, by, my

3 and 4-letter words

Short Vowel

bid, hid, kid, lid, Sid, mid, did, big, dig, fig, gig, pig, wig, rig, twig, bill, fill, ill, Jill, mill, pill, quill, till, will, bin, fin, pin, tin, win, hip, lip, nip, rip, sip, zip, bit, mitt, pit, sit, wit, zit, bib, nib, rib, crib, sib, dim, him, Jim, limb, rim, Tim, whim, miss, sis

Long vowel

eye, rye, fly, ply, spy, shy, why, cry, dry, fry, pry, try, sky

Other words

ribbon, rabbit, mittens, sibling, sister, sniff, hippo, lipstick, tiptoe, zi-pline, into, armpit, pinup, eyelid, begin, began, login, unpin, pig-pen, rip-off, bypass, myself, dry-eyed, plywood, skyline, tryout, but-terfly, blackfly, comply, outcry, sundry

Sight and memory words

farm, feed, eat, nose, ears, tail, good, ribbon, that, would, hide, barn, work, hard, pay, tea, time, line, sister, baby, needs, fish, pond, they, what, when, why where, how, who

Color words

black, amber, tan, red, emerald, green, yellow, lemon, mint, pink, indigo, cinnamon, white

Sounds and slang

eek, whoo, cluck, peep, shoo, oink, baa, meow

Canadian vs American Spelling

colour/color, axe/ax, favourite/favorite

www.ingramcontent.com/pod-product-compliance
Lightning Source LLC
Chambersburg PA
CBHW080331030726
47593CB00010B/2974

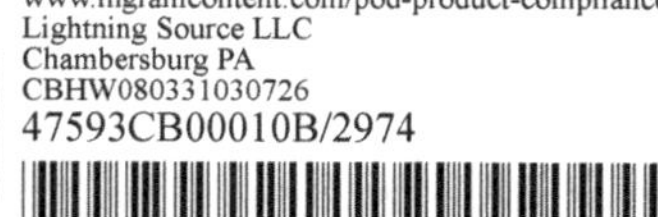